The Great Trade

-Joseph Goldsmith-

-SPECIAL THANKS-

To my good friend Brett Richter:

God has so often worked in my life through him. His love for Jesus and for people is so real – his prayers are so compassionate and powerful – his knowledge and understanding of God's Word so challenging.

He is an inspiration and an encouragement to my life.

-CONTENTS-

Forward

-FORWARD-

It seems that here in America most people say that they believe in God and in heaven. Most people consider themselves to be good people and in general most people expect that when they die they will end up in heaven. According to the words of Jesus it seems that most people are wrong in their thoughts.

Jesus said that only a few will travel the narrow road and go through the narrow gate that leads to eternal life with God - most people will not be going to heaven. Jesus said that of all those born of women there has not risen anyone greater than John the Baptist. John was the voice of introduction of Jesus as the "Lamb of God" to the people, and he baptized Jesus as a symbolic start of Jesus ministry on earth. Even Moses or King David did not have this high honor and no religious leader of today can qualify in the same way as John the Baptist did. And yet, Jesus said that the person who is least in the kingdom of heaven is greater than John.

In the days that Jesus walked the earth, the Pharisees and teachers of the law were the religious and spiritual leaders of the people. They were the equivalent of today's priests and pope, pastors and ministers, religious teachers and church leaders.

They were examples of how to live good productive lives that should be pleasing to God and certainly end with their eternity in heaven. And yet Jesus said to the people that unless their own righteousness would surpass the righteousness of their religious leaders they would certainly not be entering into heaven.

The qualifications to go to heaven are extremely high. To be with a Holy and pure God would naturally require Holiness and purity on our part as well. As I pause to think about these things I ask myself, am I in a position greater than John the Baptist? Am I more righteous than my spiritual leaders? What guarantee do I have that when I die I will go to heaven to be with God?

I believe in God. I consider myself to be a good person. I would like to be with God in heaven when I die and I would like to be assured of that in my life today.

How does a person meet the extremely high qualifications of righteousness that Jesus spoke of to enter heaven and be with God? There is of course a way for those who are willing to take part in it. God Himself has provided it. God has made - a trade.

-CHAPTER 1-

What's a Person to Do?

I realized after a little thought that it was impossible - I couldn't do it. No matter how I tried no matter who helped me - no matter how many years went by - I simply could not qualify. All my work, all my time, all my following others' directives - and still nothing. A whole lifetime of trying and I still didn't qualify. The answer was still a resounding - NO.

You wouldn't think it would be so hard - so unattainable - just to talk face to face with the President of the United States. Just to visit with him a little. Just to have a bit of a relationship with him. Not real close - just sort of a friend. You know, just to stop and see him once in a while. A cup of coffee and a little visit - that's all I wanted. The answer was - NO.

When the final word came back to my last request I sat down and started to cry a bit and think about these results. I can't have a relationship with the President of our country because I'm not the President of a different country. That's what I needed. I needed to be even with the President - on the same level - the same position. I suppose that if I had a lot of money I could donate great amounts to his campaign and then he would be my friend, then I could see him. I could sort of buy a relationship with him. I suppose that would be a sort of fake, worthless relationship in reality and anyway I don't have much money. I don't think $20 bucks to his campaign fund is going to do the trick.

So I thought - there you go - it's over - no relationship can happen. It's time to think of other things. The greatness of God came into my mind.

I've always loved the things of nature and am so often amazed at the detail and the superb design that is evident. There are 20 thousand different butterfly types, all with different color patterns and wing designs. And yet with all those to study no one knows how that caterpillar changes into a butterfly inside that chrysalis. Only God knows.

As I watch the barn swallows fly around my yard on a summer night I know they are catching mosquitoes. But how do they do that? I can't even see the mosquitoes yet they fly at great speed and catch them in midair. I don't know how that is possible, but God knows.

I live in northern Wisconsin and our winters are long and very cold and many years we have deep snow. Sometimes I'll see wild turkeys out in the fields on a day that is 20 below or perched high in a tree when the wind chill is 40 below. I could never survive in those conditions yet somehow the turkeys are there in the warmth of spring. How do they survive? I don't know - only God knows.

The other day I saw an old photo of a time in my life and I remembered with great detail that particular day. How is that possible? I can remember with great clarity something that happened forty years earlier. How is that information stored? How does this brain of mine really work? I don't know - no one does - but God knows. And my own body - I wonder sometimes how it is that my left hand always seems to know what my right hand wants to do, and it's always right there ready to help. And I think sometimes about what we used to call a simple cell of our body. And now I find that that single cell has DNA and factories and machines and endless information and tremendous unknown secrets. Now I find out that the complexity of the single building block cell of my body is greater than the sum total of the trillions of cells that make up my total body. How is that possible? That the building block can be more information rich and more complex than the total finished project? No one knows - but God knows.

God is greater than the President of the United States. The thought was heavy on my mind. I believe in God. I know God is real. I know he is great - powerful - loving. I believe Him to be perfect in every way. In ways that I'm not perfect, not even by the world's standards let alone by His standards.

Good grief, I thought. How can I ever qualify to have a relationship with this perfect God when I can't even qualify no matter what I do, or how long I try, to have a relationship with our country's President?

The thought crosses my mind that maybe this

perfect God would be willing to have a relationship with this imperfect me. You know, like a move in and stay, relationship. Close, personal - like in Heaven with him for all time - that sort of personal relationship. But then I remember the words of a wise adult to a not so wise youth, "bad company corrupts good character."[1] I knew that was a biblical truth, and I'm sure that I qualify as bad company in comparison to a perfect Holy God.   So I expect he won't, and in fact can't, compromise his good character to have a relationship with me.   For a moment a smile comes across my face - my church or some church, they can do it. They can get me in the right standing with God so that I can go to Heaven, so that I can live there with him, close and personal.   They can do it, can't they? They say they can, they say they can make me the same as God, just as pure, just as Holy, just as righteous.

I grabbed my phone and called my local law firm and asked them if they could make me President of a country so that I could be like our President and so to have a relationship with him.   You know what; they said, "yes we can."   I asked if they had a country they could give me, you know after years of doing what they say and following all their protocols, of course - NO. They didn't actually have what I needed, and they couldn't actually give me what they themselves didn't have.

If I gave all my time and effort and money to the lawyers and in the end they aren't able to do what they said after all, then I'm the one that loses everything, not them. I trusted them, they failed and I have nothing. I can see that it's extremely important to choose wisely who you put your trust in for the things of great importance in your life.

I got to thinking again about this perfect God and bad company and the churches that say we can make you perfect, we can make you so you qualify to be with this perfect God.   These churches are filled with imperfect people, imperfect leaders. Tell me I asked, if you are not perfect yourself how can you make me perfect? If you are not right with this Holy God by his standards of righteousness, then how can you make me perfect and righteous so that I qualify to have a close, personal, forever relationship with this Holy God? You can't do it - that I am positive. Church membership and doing church things probably makes me a better person in this world but it does not make me as pure and Holy as our God.

One thing I know, I can't give someone something I don't have.   It doesn't matter if it's a chocolate chip cookie or a Rolls Royce, if I don't have it I can't give it to someone else. And doing all this stuff you want me to do to be able to qualify - well, when I look at the extremely high standard of Holiness and purity of righteousness that is God's standard, I can do stuff until the end of my days and I'm still bad company compared to this good God.   In the end, I find I'm no closer to having a meaningful relationship with God than I am with the President of the U.S.

So what's a person to do? I decided the best thing to do was to consult God myself about this relationship thing.   I had tried to consult with the President but could not. But with God, we have His words written down. We can read and study the Bible. I wanted to find out myself what God has to say about all this. After all, it's Him I want to know, Him I want the personal relationship with, Him I want to spend my eternal life with. After all, my question is not that hard. I know that bad company corrupts good character, and I know I'm bad company. I also know God can't lower His standards and become bad company like me in order to have a personal relationship. That would make God not perfect, not perfectly holy, and not perfectly righteous.

The conclusion isn't all that difficult. All that's required is to make me "good company." You know, it's like make me a President of a country, and then I can call up the President of the U.S. and he will talk to me. So with God all I need is to be made "good company," you know, just as pure, just as holy, and just as righteous as He is. Then I can be right there with Him - Him with me, me with Him, almost as one together.

So God, how do I become as you are? How do I become as pure - as Holy - as righteous as you are? How do I do that? I decided to take a look in my Bible.

I was wondering if doing good in my life would make me righteous before God. You know, live life doing more good than evil. Is that what it takes? And of course believing in God, and I do believe in God and in Heaven.

I came across this scripture - Matthew 7:21 - Jesus is talking and He says, "Not everyone who says to me

Lord, Lord, will enter the Kingdom of Heaven, but only he who does the will of My Father who is in Heaven." I looked at that scripture and read it over and over. People who say Lord, Lord, they believe in God. These are religious people. And that word ONLY - that's a powerful word. "Only he who does the will of the Father." Do I really know - know for sure the will of the Father? Yet the scripture says only these people go to heaven.

It is of interest to note that nowhere could I find in my Bible that the will of the Father was for me to rely on a membership in some particular religious group, following their teachings and traditions as a way to get into heaven.

In Matthew 7:13-14 I know that Jesus is talking about getting into Heaven. "Enter through the narrow gate," He says. "For wide is the gate and broad is the road that leads to destruction and many enter through it. But small is the gate and narrow the road that leads to life, and only a few find it."

Jesus says that only a few find the correct path - the correct gate that gets you into Heaven. That's the path that I want, the gate that I'm looking for. Only a few find it. Well, I want to be part of that few!

I notice in Matthew 8:11-12, Jesus says, "I say to you that many will come from the East and the West and will take their place at the feast with Abraham, Isaac and Jacob in the Kingdom of Heaven, but the subjects of the kingdom will be thrown outside, into the darkness where there will be weeping and gnashing of teeth."

I know Jesus is referring to entering Heaven when he says these things. As would be expected, the enemies of the kingdom are not allowed in and those who live and reside in the kingdom but are not really citizens would not be allowed in.   But this also says that the subjects of the kingdom, that's the good citizens who know the king, that follow the laws of the kingdom and even help support the kingdom with taxes and things. The subjects of the kingdom are thrown outside. They're excluded and not allowed in either.

I know the feeling, when I tried to get in to see the President I told them that I was a good citizen, paid my taxes and followed the laws of the country. Always praised the President and supported him fully.   They threw me out. And yes there was some weeping and gnashing of teeth. This is what it's like with God? My question to God – 'who got to go in?' I want to be in that group.

-CHAPTER 2-

What Does God Say About This?

I needed to start at the beginning, Genesis Chapter 1, "God created the heavens and the earth."[2] Why? That's easy to see from science. Everything is all set up for man to live here. The design is for us to live and grow and increase. And then God created man, Adam and Eve.

It says in Luke 3:38 that Adam was God's son. Think of that, Adam was God's son. So Eve was God's daughter. His children. Created by Him - created in His likeness. Alive in their spirits as God is spirit. They were able to walk and talk and have a great personal relationship with their Dad. Living in a wonderful place. Adam and Eve were good company to our perfect God. And of course, why not. God created them so naturally he created them perfect.

Perfectly righteous in all ways, perfectly sin free, good company for Himself.

I hadn't thought about it until now, with the President of the U.S., I could have a relationship with him, close, personal, lasting, loving - if I was his son, and if I wanted the relationship and if he wanted the relationship. For any relationship to be real you have to be able to choose, to choose if you want the relationship or not. If you don't have choice the relationship is forced, it's fake. You must have free will to decide on your own if you want to love someone or not; to share your life with someone or not; even to obey or not.

When God created Adam and Eve, He created them with free will. They could follow His wishes and do as He asked, or not. Chapter 3 of Genesis is the fall of man. Adam and Eve were created pure - holy - righteous - good company for God, but they disobeyed God.[3] They chose to disobey, they chose to sin. Sin is unrighteousness. It is not correct with God. It is not holy, not pure. It is corrupted from God's way. It is not good company for God. So Adam and Eve's sin caused them to fall alright - they fell from a position of purity and righteousness with God, sin free, to a place of corruption and unrighteousness with God.

Their relationship with God in the way that God intended it to be was over. They were forced from the garden they lived in and out into the world. As I read through the next chapters I see that things are going very bad. God wants righteous people, sin free people, so that He can have a relationship with them. But to be in a real relationship the people have to have free will, to choose for themselves. And the people do choose. They choose not just for themselves, but they choose themselves. They choose themselves first - selfishness. They don't live with their spirit in tune with God's spirit anymore. They live with their very nature, selfish. A very nature toward sin. A very nature against God. The whole world ends up corrupt and sinful but God still wants that close personal relationship with His created people so He picks out one man and his family who seem pretty good and He decides to clear the rest of the earth of its corruption, and start all over again.

It's in Genesis chapters 5-9, Noah and the flood. But it seems it doesn't take long and the whole world is corrupt again. God doesn't give up, he picks Abraham. It starts in Genesis 12. God decides to make his own nation among the world of people. These would be His chosen people, a special righteous nation and He would be their God, and they would be His people. We all know the story of the Israelite slaves in Egypt and how Moses came and led them for 40 years in the desert and then Joshua took them into the Promised Land.[4] They started out pretty good, not great, not God's quality of righteousness but a little more righteous as they tried to follow God's laws for them. So they were a little better company for God and He could get a little closer to them. Remember how God dwelled in the temple - with the ark of God. But the people had free will and their very nature was toward selfishness, toward sin and away from God.

In the end that great nation was lost and there was nothing left but a few remnants living in foreign countries.   And now, what of all the people of the world - all the people with their free will and selfish sinful nature?   Paul tells us the truth in Romans 1:29-32, "They have become filled with every kind of wickedness, evil, greed and depravity.   They are full of envy, murder, strife, deceit and malice.   They are gossips, slanderers, God haters, insolent, arrogant and boastful.   They invent ways of doing evil, they disobey their parents, are senseless, fruitless, heartless, and ruthless. Although they know God's righteous decree that those who do such things deserve death, they not only continue to do these very things but also approve of those who practice them."

And in Romans 3:23 Paul writes, "For all have sinned and fall short of the glory of God."   This is where we are. What must be the thoughts of God? He creates a world and creates people to love and care for and He gives them free will so that they can genuinely love Him.   He wants sons and daughters that obey Him and become like He is but the people choose to follow themselves instead. They choose selfishness and so to live by their sin nature, their flesh, not their spirit as God had intended.   No one righteous, no one sin free - not one. No sons, no daughters, no good company for God. As it says in Romans 6:23, all the people are deserving of death because, "The wages of sin is death."

If the purpose of your creation was to have a close personal relationship with God and your sin prevents that, your value to God is pretty much gone. Starting the world over again with Noah, then trying a separate nation with Israel and God even gave an offer to Moses to make a new nation from him as we see in Exodus 32:10. But Moses thought it a bad idea so he talked Him out of it. And now the whole world is bad. The whole world sinful. The very nature of man to be sinful, the very nature of man to be selfish.

All of the commandments and all of the laws that the Israelites had to help them to live righteous before God seemed mostly to show them how sinful they were. Their special status as God's chosen nation - their prophets and priests - their special sacrifices and religious traditions could not get them pure and holy before God. No one was in a position to have the fullness of the relationship that God desired. No one qualified for heaven on his own good works.

I have noticed that parents spend considerable time trying to teach their children to share, but they never have to spend a moment to teach them to be selfish. Selfishness is strong and full in any 3 year old, it's built right in, they're born with it. Born with a selfish nature, born with a heart towards themselves and so towards evil and away from God.

It looks pretty obvious to me - man can't do it. Man can't get man right with God. I can't get myself right with God if this is my very nature to be sinful. And some church group or leader can't get me right with God either. First of all, how can one sinner get another sinner cleaned up? And besides, the standards of righteousness are God's standards. Not the church's, not the world's, not man's standards, not my standards but God's perfect standards.   I can't do it - and no man can do it for me. That I know is fact.   I need all my sins from the past paid for and forgiven.   I need new perfect righteousness.   I need a new nature, not living by my sin nature but to get back to the way Adam and Eve were in the beginning when they were happy with God, living by their spirits. Their spirits with God's spirit - good company. I need to be a son. A son of God. That's what I need to be. I need all those things taken care of so that I am right with God. And I need to be a true honest son of God to have the inheritance of heaven. I can't just do these things. I can't just be His son, no one can, and no church, no priest, no pastor, no man can accomplish this feat for me.

But wait a minute I thought, there must be a way. There are lots of churches out there that seem pretty convinced that if I go to their church I should certainly end up in heaven when I die.   And I believe that the churches, at least many of them, do help people to know God through Jesus Christ and to live good productive lives. I find in my Bible that God says it's important for His people to meet together as groups for many reasons.   So the churches are important if they honor God in what they teach and do.

As I read in my Bible the words as "only a few" and "only those who do the Father's will" and "the subjects are locked out" I am a bit concerned about just being a member of a church.   It seems that there are some people who will be going to heaven in many or perhaps most of the churches. But also there will be many people in the churches who will not be going to heaven even though they think that they will be.

What I want to know is, what's the difference? Why do some in the same church get to go to heaven and some do not? God's words in the Bible are very restrictive. It seems a few here - a few there - more here - less there. I don't like not knowing until after I die. That's too late to make changes. I want to know now. And I want a down payment in advance just to be absolutely sure.

-CHAPTER 3-

A New Perspective

I wonder if I have been thinking in too short of terms. Perhaps I need to think more long term, you know kind of like a payment plan. Perhaps like buying a house, you pay for 30 years and then you own the house - except for me. I must have done something wrong as I'm past my 30 years of payments and I still don't own my house. So there might be a few extra hoops to jump through, but with help perhaps after a lifetime I'll be in heaven at the end, and that's all I want.

Let's see, rules to follow, membership to maintain, money to give, being good and not bad, I can do those things and then I will be right with God, good company – right?

Well I felt pretty good about all those things, just pick out a church, become a member in good standing, live a good life (and that I wanted to do anyway) and give some money. Of course that part had me a bit concerned. Oh, I wanted to give some money to the church, but how much? You know, where is the amount that qualifies you with God, without, you know, excess. Generosity is good but I do have to live after all. If I die before my house mortgage is paid in full, well that's the way it goes, but what if I die before I've paid my full amount due to the church?

My thoughts went back to my money donated to the president's reelection fund, how much do I have to give before he becomes my friend? I can't answer that but I know it's more money than I will ever have - and with God, He owns this world so isn't my money sort of His already. So, all these things are my way of trying to be good, to be pleasing to God, to be His friend. Gosh - look what happened. I'm back trying to earn my relationship with God, or even worse I think, to buy my relationship with God. Good grief - if I could earn it or if I could buy it - my relationship with God - it must not be worth much. I know better than that, we're talking the creator of the stars here, the creator of life itself. I am well convinced as I see the things He has created that there is nothing greater than knowing Him and being with Him now and forever.

As I said, I'm asking God how to have a relationship with Him, so I went back to my Bible. Interestingly I came across a scripture in Romans, "No one is found righteous by observing the law."[5] The law was the way the Jews - that was God's chosen nation - tried to be good. They tried to do good works to be right with God. They wanted to be able to be closer to God, to be even with his perfection so they could have that perfect relationship with God. So they did good works and followed the law as best they could. "No one is found righteous by observing the law," that means no one qualifies for heaven by observing the law. That doesn't leave any room for someone to slip quietly into heaven undetected just because he is a good person. I came across another scripture, "All my good works are like filthy rags in the eyes of God."[6] Gosh.

No one is found righteous and the penalty for sin is death - that's me. I can't earn this relationship. I don't deserve it. I can't buy it and the church doesn't have it either because they're just like me - sinners. So they can't give it to me. At least I know now that the people who join the churches, live good lives, follow the laws and rules set up by God and man and give to their churches and other places, at least I know now that these things do not get them right with God. These things do not qualify them for a relationship with God. The people who do those things of good works hopefully do them for a different reason than to try to get themselves into heaven.

So why do they do these things? I'll have to think about that a bit more. My thoughts returned to something much more important to me, and that was getting into heaven - to get to be with God forever. I've learned something now, something very important. No matter what I do myself, or how hard I try I cannot qualify for a personal relationship with this most Holy and pure God. And no one can get me qualified because they don't qualify either and so they can't give me something they don't have. And as far as the

President of the United States goes it's the same thing. I am not the President's son, so I don't qualify for a relationship with him that way, and all my good works and money won't do the trick either. None of the people that I know qualify to be with the president so they can't somehow give me something that they don't have themselves. If we were talking about God here the people I know are just like me also - sinners - unrighteous sinners.

So everything seems impossible, except - but wait, this sounds a bit strange, but think, the President qualifies to be with the President. He qualifies to be with himself right? So couldn't he, the President himself, somehow qualify me? Qualify me to be with him, to know him, to be like a son to him. Couldn't he do this himself, for me? In fact it's the only thing that would work, if he did it, if he qualified me, if he made me right.

Let's see. The President would have to want to do that and I'm not sure if he would or why he would, but that's first. He would have to want to see me, to know me and wish that we could spend time together. He would have to OK everything with the secret service and the FBI. And the local guards would have to know and have the OK to let me in, and there would be a lot of other hard things to do.

I think if I could, I would just ask the President if he would send someone special to sort of pick me up. You know, like a special escort to get me through all the checkpoints and guards. Someone I could just sort of stick tight to. Someone who already qualifies to go

all the way in to see the President and then I would just
stay close to this guy. I could use all his security passes
and entry privileges. I could just walk right in just like I
belong there, just like as if I was the President's real
son. If I just hang on tight to my special agent, I'm in.
I'm in to see the President. And it's all because the
President himself wanted me there. He qualified me
himself and he sent someone for me to attach to, and
so now I can go through all the security to be with him.

I figured it out. I know the one and only way for
me to be with the President. He makes me right to be
with him. He clears the way. I accept his offer to come
to be with him and so he sends someone who already
qualifies to be with him to get me, and bring me
through.

It's the only way it will work, except for one thing.
The President doesn't know me. He doesn't want to
know me, and he doesn't want me to be like a son to
him. So he won't make me right with him to know
him and he won't clear the way and he won't send
someone for me to attach to so I can use his credentials
to enter the White House. Shucks - that ends that.
But wait, it's not really the President that I want to
know or be with, it's God. The creator. That perfect
and Holy one. That's really who I want to know and
spend eternity with.

As I've been thinking about the President I've
learned some things about me having a relationship
with God. First, I can't qualify myself to be with God,
and no person or church is righteous enough before
God so that they can give me the perfection in my spirit

that I need. No one and no church can make me right -
get rid of my sins that make me deserving of death
instead of heaven with God. No one or no church can
give me the righteousness, the perfectness of God
himself so that I qualify because they themselves don't
have it and they can't give me something they don't
already have. And working for perfect righteousness is
nothing but a false hope and a joke.

Second, there is a way that I can be with God, a way
that I can go to heaven, a way that I can be made right
in His eyes. A way that I can pass through that narrow
gate and be with God.   It's like getting in to see the
President. God has to do it. He has to qualify me. He
has to make me right. He has to open the doors. He
has to send someone so I can use that person's access
to God as my own access to God.   God has to do all
these things and more, and like going to see the
President, all I have to do - all I can do in fact - is
accept His offer.

So I've made my decision. I want to know God. I
want to see Him. I want to be with Him in my eternity
and even right now.   I have free will and my will is to
know God closely - personally - permanently.   Now
God has free will also, so does He wish to know me?
Yes - yes for sure.   He created us for the express
purpose that he may have a loving relationship with us.
And over and over again in our Bible, like with Noah
and Abraham, He keeps trying to work things out so
that we can come to know Him forever if we want to.

You might ask why, why does God want to know
me and you?   The answer is love. God created us to

love Him and for Him to love us. In fact, in the book of John he shows us just how strong is this quality of God. John says, "God is love."[7] He is the essence of love, the very source of love. I know John 3:16, "For God so loved the world that he gave his one and only Son, that whoever shall believe on Him shall not perish but have eternal life." God loved the people of the world so much that He sent His only Son so that we may know Him and be with Him, much like the President sending a special agent with access privilege to himself and then to just bring me on into his presence.

But wait - God Himself is pure - holy - sinless - perfect in ways of God that man cannot even approach. These things are no problem with going in to see the President because he is just a man. Not holy, not sin free, not perfect, the same as me. I could go in to see him just the way I am. But God - the Holy Creator - that's a different story. I'm not good company for God in the sinful condition that I'm in. Jesus has to bring me in but He must make me perfectly righteous first. He must make me able to stand in the presence of this Holy God. And like Paul wrote in Romans, "All have sinned and fall short of the glory of God."[8] That's me. I have sinned and fall short of the glory of God. I cannot be in God's presence in the condition that I'm in.

It sure looks like God sent Jesus to get me, to bring me to heaven, to get me through the narrow gate. But first of all can He do that? Does He have the right credentials? Remember, you can't give something you don't have.   Let's see, Jesus is God's Son, we know that. He is sin free, never sinned so Holy and righteous before God.   So He does have access to God, in person, in heaven, but that's Him. He can stand before God, righteous and His Son, but what of me? Jesus can't just get me in like the special agent because when I get there I'm still a sinner, still unrighteous, still deserving of death, eternal death, eternal separation from God.   So Jesus can't just grab my hand and bring me on in like the special agent could.   I can't stand before God without being perfect - perfectly holy, perfectly righteous.

I already know that no man and no church can make me this perfectness of righteousness. They don't have it - I can't earn it - they can't give me what they don't have. I know all that from before.   Only God can do what needs to be done. And let's see, what does need to be done so that I can know Him and be with Him now and forever?

I know that God is spirit and when I die my flesh rots in the ground. I know I was created a spirit being and it is my spirit that goes to be with God. So of course it is the condition of my spirit that is of greatest concern.   So I need to be pure and righteous in my spirit, sin free here. God cannot be around sin, but I have sinned and there is a death penalty for that, my spirit separated from God forever. That penalty has to be paid, that separation from God fulfilled. God needs to do this. And I need to be pure and holy. I need to be righteous before God, God's perfect standard of righteousness before Him, and God needs to do this.

And I need a different relationship to God, because right now as a sinner and unrighteous I am more like an enemy to God than a friend.   And the kingdom of God is always spoken of as an inheritance, so I need the closest relationship I can have.   I need to be His son. Yes - I need to be God's son and only God can do that part also.

And I know I need to get back to living by my spirit. My spirit, in touch with the spirit of God, so I can have that relationship and know his love and become more like him.   I need help to stop living my sin life, and my very nature to sin needs to be redone back to living by my spirit.   I need to be sort of starting over - spirit in control this time. And I need His help to do all these things. And oh yes, remember I said I want to know, to know if I am going to heaven.   I want something like an assurance, a bit of a down payment of what's to come perhaps, and God needs to do that also.

I look at all these things that must be done for me or you to really know God and to really be with God and I can't do any of them.   God Himself has to do it all for me.   I look at myself and I look at my life and it seems so much to ask of the creator of all things - will you do all these things for me? Will you forgive my sins - pay my penalty - give me the holiness and righteousness of spirit that you as God Himself has? Will you help me, and recreate me, so that I can live by my spirit instead of my flesh? Will you call me your son and qualify me for your inheritance of heaven? Will you do all these things and more? I am deserving of nothing except to pay my own penalty for my sins - that's death - separation from God forever.   Will you do all this for me - for a sinner - just because you love me?

I think at this point as I ponder these questions in my mind, that if God will do all these things just so that I can know Him and become like Him, the love that is in this God for me is greater and stronger than anything I can understand.   It is pure, Holy, and totally unconditional, as I know what I have earned from God and it's not His love.

I find as I think these thoughts that I want to know this God even more, deeper and more real than before. This is not a God who wants to catch me doing something wrong and send me to hell. This is a God who wants to love me and bring me to heaven.

-CHAPTER 4-

The Trade

Does God really want to love me and bring me to heaven? Does God really want to love you and bring you to heaven? Is this His heart, is this His will, am I thinking things correctly?

Let me see, what does God have? You know, with the people all sinful because all have sinned and fall short of the glory of God.

When Jesus was here on the earth, He had Jesus. He was His son. He was perfectly righteous. Sin free and able to be in God's presence and to have the perfect relationship with God the Father. And God had the people of the world. None were righteous so none could have the relationship with God. None were sons. None qualified for the inheritance of heaven. So God had Jesus on one side, a son, righteous, sin free, a perfect relationship. On the other side was me, you and everyone else, not sons, not righteous, sinful, no close relationship.

But look again at John 3:16, it says, for God so loved the world that He gave his son Jesus - He gave His son Jesus? I know that when Jesus hung on the cross just before He died He spoke to God in heaven and said, "My God, My God, why have you forsaken me?" [9] I'm sure Jesus knew the answer because Jesus knew everything. He spoke those words so that I might think about them and ask the same question. Father God, why did you forsake your son Jesus? The word "forsake" is a strong word, it means to abandon, to disown, not just to turn your back on but to claim you are no longer my son.

Father God did this. His love was so strong for the people of the world that He gave Jesus - He gave up His son Jesus. God made a choice. A decision. The people of the world - or Jesus. Some sort of a trade. He had Jesus. He didn't have the people of the world. But if He made a trade, Jesus for the people of the world, then He won't have Jesus - but He will have, or can have, the people of the world.

Is God willing to make this Great Trade for me, for you, for anyone who will take Him up on this trade? The thought is amazing. His love is so great for the people. His sacrifice so high for us sinners. If my thoughts are correct and God has made this trade it is the greatest trade ever made. The most important. The most lasting. Requiring the greatest sacrifice and the greatest love.   And salvation itself is completely dependent on this trade that God Himself makes. If you take part in this trade you become a son or daughter of God with all its benefits and responsibilities, and a spot in heaven is prepared for you. If you do not take part in this trade then you are on your own, attempting to get into heaven by your own good works, and you know what that will bring to you.

This is of extreme great importance. A trade that God makes, where he trades His son for the people of the world. The perfectness of His son for the sinfulness of man. I decided I want to find that written down in my Bible for me to read and study, to think about and understand. I want to make that trade. I find my love for God increasing as I see His love for me. I want to love this God who loves me. I want to know Him, be like Him, and worship Him. I want to serve Him, honor Him, and obey Him. I want to give Him my life. I want to be His son.

2 Corinthians 5:21 - The Great Trade, I found it, it's there. It's written down by God for us to read. It says, "God made Him who had no sin to be sin for us, so that in Him we might become the righteousness of God."

Read that scripture and then read it again, look what it says, "God made," God, Father God, He's the one in charge. He's the one making the trade. He has the power and authority. He's the one taking the initiative. "God made," God Himself is doing it and as I learned before, there is no other way. God has to do this. No church, no man, no priest or good person can make this trade. Only God Himself can and must do this if we are to know His love and love Him as He wants things to be.

So God made Him who had no sin - who's that? Jesus of course! We already know all of mankind has sinned. Only Jesus was sin free. Only Jesus was a Son of God. Only Jesus was perfectly righteous before God, and only Jesus had God's actual righteousness. So God made Jesus who was sin free to be sin for us. He gave Jesus our sin. Father God took our sin and gave it to His perfect sin free Son. And then what? And why? So that we can be in Him, that is, in Jesus – "in Christ" - joined to Christ - hooked up to Christ. It's sort of like hooking up to our special agent except that with Jesus remember we are talking spirit. God is spirit, and our spirit wants to be with God. If we are hooked to Jesus, "in Christ," we are hooked together in our very spirits.

The special agent takes me by the hand - Jesus takes me by the spirit. My spirit held by His spirit and look at what's been done. It says so that in Him - "in Christ"- we might become the righteousness of God. Just think about that, we might become the righteousness of God. Perfect God righteousness. Perfect "standing in the presence of God" righteousness. We might become this. Do you see what a great thing Father God is doing here? Do you understand? Look again, think about what it says. "God made Him who had no sin to be sin for us, so that in Him we might become the righteousness of God." A trade has occurred, a great most wonderful trade has occurred and God has done it. He himself has made it. He gave my sins to sin free Jesus and the perfect righteousness that Jesus has to me.

Remember, Jesus has God righteousness. God quality, not world quality righteousness. Jesus and only Jesus has perfect God righteousness. This is the only righteousness that qualifies to be with God. To stand in His presence and to be with Him forever. Only Jesus has it, God righteousness, and only God can give it to us and then only if we desire it and request it. We always have free will. We always have a choice.

If you give my sins to Jesus He is no longer perfect and so He loses His perfect God quality righteousness. So Father God took Jesus' righteousness and gave it to us. To those who want it. To those who will accept it. A trade, a Great Trade, a powerful wonderful trade. My sins to Jesus, Jesus' righteousness to me. And all the world's sins to Jesus and Jesus' righteousness to anyone who joins up with Jesus. It's for anyone who becomes "in Him" as it says "in Christ." If we are "in Christ," the trade is made. Our sins to Jesus and with them, for Jesus, the penalty of death and separation from God that they demand, and Jesus' righteousness to us, and the opportunity to know God and be with God now and forever.

Look what has happened. God had Jesus as a Son, perfect, sin free and righteous before Him. The perfect relationship. And He had you and me, the people of the world. Not sons, not sin free, not righteous before God, and no close relationship could occur. But even when the people were sinners God so loved the world. He loved Jesus too, of course. But He loved the world, the people He created and He wanted them to be with

Him, to know Him and to love Him.

And Jesus loved the people of the world also and so our perfect and innocent Jesus chose to take for himself the pain and punishment that our sin demands. Your sin and my sin. Jesus agreed to carry our punishment to His cross and to His grave. And so God Himself made the Great Trade. The people of the world for Jesus. And now Jesus is full of sin, my sin, your sin, His righteousness gone, a great penalty to pay - separation from God. More than a physical separation, a spiritual separation from God, and death required for all the sins. Blood to shed. A cross to be executed on. A sonship to be eliminated. And Jesus' dying words "why have you forsaken me?" Words for us to think about, Jesus asking Father God, why am I no longer your son? Why am I separated from you? Why am I covered with sin? Why is your wrath and anger directed towards me? Why do I die on this cross? We should ask these things ourselves. Why did Jesus have to die this way? Why this separation from Father God? Why this Great Trade?

The answer is quite easy. There is no other way possible. No way that man can qualify for himself to be with this perfect God. If there were any other way - a church - good deeds - money - a pope - a place like purgatory - a special church sacrifice for sins, anything, any other way possible and Jesus never would have had to die on a cross. He never would have had to give up His own righteousness to the people who want it. He never would have had to lose His position as a Son of God to people who want to be God's sons or daughters. If there was any other way possible without God trading His Son Jesus for us, Jesus never would have died on a cross, full of sin and separated from God. But God knew. He knows man and He knows His own perfectness and He knew that He Himself would have to make it possible for man to know Him and to love Him and to be with Him. Before the creation of the world - before there was man on earth, God knew.[10] He knew He would have to pay for the people's sins and furnish the needed perfect righteousness to them. He knew He would have to make all these things available to all the people if He was going to have a close personal relationship with at least some of them.

Remember, to love someone, really love them and want them in your life you must have free will, free will to choose yes or no, and God made man with free will. So, as it says in 2 Corinthians 5:21, "We might become the righteousness of God" - or we might not, depending on us, on our choice. God has done His part. He has made it possible for us to know Him and love Him and be with Him now and forever. But if we have free will we can choose, we can choose to accept the Great Trade, to become in Him, "in Christ," a righteous son of God, or we can choose not to. We have free will, we have a choice.

I say again - how great is the love of God for us. A love so deep, so powerful, so pure and unconditional. This God, this God of eternity, creator of trillions of stars and He has a love for us so deep so lasting that He wants us to be His very children.

The apostle John was helping us to understand our creator when he wrote in 1 John 3:1, "How great is the love the Father has lavished on us, that we should be called children of God! And that is what we are!" The driving force - the power behind all the things of God is love. Yes love. His goal, His commitment, His purpose for your existence is all to love you and have you love Him, now and forever.

How different from our world. It seems so much of the world runs on selfishness, greed, power over others and fear of punishment. And then there is God who makes His decisions always based on love. That doesn't mean He controls us, that wouldn't be love. That doesn't mean He makes us know Him, choose Him and love Him, that wouldn't be love. And that doesn't mean you have no part in your own destiny, or your own eternity, that wouldn't be love. And that doesn't mean He ignores our wrong acts, our sins, that wouldn't be love either. After all, if you love your own child you teach them and direct them and in ways you live in them and through them as they take on your own values and integrity.

God is no different with His children. If you see a child who needs direction in their life but you are not their parent, there are a few things you can do to try to influence that child but there's not the same opportunity and responsibility as you have with your own children. God is just the same. Some are His children, some are not. He does what He can, loving all of them always, but never taking away their free will to choose.

-CHAPTER 5-

A Step Back

I decided I needed to take a step back, to slow down a bit, to relook at this "Great Trade," to check out other areas of my Bible to see if I could find evidence that my thoughts were correct. I wanted to be sure. I wanted to know this God of love. This God who would love me so much that He wanted me to be His son, yet also loved me so much that He would let me choose to be away from Him now and forever. I decided to look around to see what I could see.

I remember my readings in Matthew 7:13 where Jesus says, "Enter through the narrow gate for wide is the gate and broad is the road that leads to destruction and many enter through it. But small is the gate and narrow the road that leads to life, and only a few find it." Jesus is telling us that not everyone is going to Heaven, in fact most people will be on the wide road and will go to destruction and not to life. Jesus says that only a few travel the narrow road, only a few enter through the small gate. Certainly salvation is not automatic. That would go against the will of many people, and we remember that being with God is called an inheritance and we know an inheritance goes to the children.[11] No wonder there's such an emphasis on being a child of God.

It's interesting that here in Matthew, Jesus says to enter through the narrow gate, the gate that few choose to enter through and in John 10:7 I find that Jesus says, "I am the gate." Jesus says He is the gate and you must enter through Him to have life.

In John 1:12-13, John is writing about Jesus and he says, "Yet to all who received Him (Jesus) to those who believed in His name, He gave the right to become children of God - children born not of natural decent, nor of human decision or a husband's will, but born of God." Yes, it says born of God. Not just in thought. Not even just in faith, but really born of God. How can that be?

In John chapter 3, a man named Nicodemus came to Jesus and asked Him about entering the kingdom of God. Jesus told him in verse 3, "I tell you the truth, no one can see the kingdom of God unless he is born again." And in verse 5, Jesus says to Nicodemus, "I tell you the truth, no one can enter the kingdom of God unless he is born of water and the spirit. Flesh gives birth to flesh but the spirit gives birth to spirit."

Nicodemus was a very smart man and he knew he would have to be right with God to enter the Kingdom of Heaven. He knew that water was a way to clean you up, at least on the outside. And he knew that he needed cleaning on the inside as well. Reborn on the inside sort of speaking, clean and pure. And we know that the Great Trade provides for that inside cleaning as we can't ever clean ourselves up sufficiently on the inside to be like God. But the trade, the trade makes available for us the very righteousness of Jesus Himself. Now that's being reborn of pure water, pure righteousness. Nicodemus understood that part but what about this born of the spirit? Is there even more to this Great Trade than I know?

Romans 8:1 says, "Therefore, there is now no condemnation for those who are in Christ Jesus." And Romans 6:23 says, "For the wages of sin is death, but the gift of God is eternal life in Christ Jesus our Lord." In Christ Jesus our Lord, that's what it says. I know that I can't be with God because of my sins. I have earned death, that's what I deserve. But the gift of God, the gift from God is eternal life in Christ Jesus. God gives to me a gift. But it isn't just a gift from God but it is actually a gift "of" God as well. That's what makes it so special. I know that if I make the Great Trade, God has given my sins to Jesus and His righteousness to me. But there's more than that, much deeper than that. I can tell - as my sins are given to Jesus, I am given to Jesus. I am somehow spiritually in a God way now "in Christ," in Jesus. I am sure of this because scripture verifies it for me. It says in Romans 6:5, "If we have been united with Him (Jesus) like this in His death, we will certainly also be united with Him in His resurrection."

It says united with Him. Not just our sins given to Him in this trade but us united with Him. In Galatians

2:20 it says, "I have been crucified with Christ and I no longer live, but Christ lives in me. The life I live in the body, I live by faith in the Son of God, who loved me and gave himself for me." I have been crucified with Christ. I can see why Nicodemus had a little trouble with this part. But God is spirit and I am spirit. The real me the inside part, the part that can be with God for eternity, that's my spirit not my body. So in a way, my sins have destroyed my spirit so it can't be with God. My spirit needs to be washed clean - yes - as reborn with pure righteousness - pure clean water – Jesus' pure clean righteousness. But then my spirit needs to live again, it needs life as my sin has earned it death. So I now live by my flesh and not by my spirit - my spirit needs new life. I need to be born again - my spirit needs to be born again. So if I make the Great Trade I am then "in Christ" in a spiritual way - in a God way.

I like the words we read in Romans 8:1, "There is now no condemnation for those who are in Christ." That's me if I make the trade. I'm not condemned for my sins; they're all taken care of - on the cross. Jesus took them and so He took me to His cross. I was crucified with Christ.

So now, if I make the Great Trade I am "in Christ." I am spiritually attached to Jesus, yet I know that my own spirit must be born again, it must have new life. I know that I have Jesus' own righteousness as my own righteousness, but there's more yet in this trade. I found it in Romans chapter 8. Chapter 8 verse 9 says, "You however are controlled not by the sinful nature but by the spirit, if the spirit of God lives in you. And if anyone does not have the spirit of Christ, he does not belong to Christ." Verse 10, "But if Christ is in you, your body is dead because of sin, yet your spirit is alive because of righteousness."

Do you see what this says? You are controlled by the spirit, not the flesh. Not the sin nature side but by the spirit. But not just by my spirit alone but by the spirit of God with my spirit. As my spirit is given to Jesus and I am "in Christ" in the same way - at the trade – Jesus' spirit is given to me to be with my spirit. That brings new life to my spirit. It is reborn. Christ is in me, His spirit with my spirit - and I am in Him, my spirit with His spirit.

2 Corinthians 5:17 says, "Therefore, if anyone is in Christ, he is a new creation, the old has gone, the new has come!" I am truly born again.   My spirit is alive because Jesus' spirit is with my spirit, attached together as one and Jesus' spirit is alive. And His spirit lives forever - pure, Holy, God righteous, and so my spirit is alive forever - pure, Holy, God righteous.

My spirit with Jesus' spirit is now back in control, not my flesh, not my sin nature. I have new life in my spirit. I can know God. I can be with Him and He can be with me. He can and does actually live in me. His spirit, Jesus' spirit, together with my spirit. I am now a Son of God. I qualify for the inheritance of heaven, yes, but there is so much more. I am now able to have the true, pure, Holy, intimate relationship with God that I was created by Him to have. I can love Him and experience His love for me just as Jesus loved His

Father and knew His Father's love for Him. The trade, the Great Trade. All because of the Great Trade.

And there's more - with Jesus' spirit with my spirit there is power over sin - power to live righteous.[12] There's a wanting to do good things, not to become righteous before God, but because we now are righteous before God. Right from my very spirit there is a wanting to love God. A wanting to serve Him, to glorify Him, to honor Him. A wanting to live with integrity, to serve righteousness and live it, instead of selfishness and sin. It's not just a change. It's indeed a rebirth, a new creation, a change in my very nature. And God did it. He did it all. He made the trade. He provided the way and He never took away my free will. My will to say 'yes' or my will to say 'no.' He never took away my choice to try and gain righteousness before God by my own means, like being a good person or through a church membership or special sacrifice. He never took away all the countless ways that people try to earn righteousness with God. God simply provided for us the only way that will ever work to be righteous before Him, and we can choose that way - or attempt some other way - or we can have nothing to do with any of it. We have free will. God never takes that away from us.

Love - I say again all this because of love. Pure - Holy - uncompromising - unconditional - love. A love that gives all on God's part, but yet also a God that cannot be this great loving God and compromise who He is, or the qualifications required to be with him.

We know now the qualifications to go to heaven to

be with a perfect righteous God. In our spirits we must be as God is - perfectly righteous. And the penalty of death for our sins must be paid.

When we are joined with Jesus in spirit, we are one with Him at the cross and the penalty for our sins is paid, and we have His righteousness. If we are joined with Jesus now - we are joined with God in heaven, forever.

I look at these things and am amazed. It makes perfect sense. It's the only way. The qualifications to go to heaven are not unexpected - to be with a Holy God needs to require Holiness in us. And that no church, pastor, priest, purgatory, sacrifice, membership or money can qualify you only makes common sense. The qualifications are too high for man to achieve them himself. Jesus is the way. Jesus is the only way.

-CHAPTER 6-

The Father's Will

I feel a relief in my heart. I understand things now. God's perfect love for me, the Great Trade. But wait - what about that part in Matthew 7:21, remember, "Not everyone will go to heaven but only those who do the will of my Father who is in heaven." I think about this scripture again and the restrictive quality of that word "only." I think it is easy to predict what the will of the Father is concerning all of us. After all, we were created by Him to know Him, to love Him and to know His love for us. Created to be with Him now and forever and we know that is not possible if we are not "in Christ." We must be hooked to Jesus, having Jesus' spirit with our spirit, having Jesus' very righteousness for our own. So what would be the Father's will? Of course, He would want us to come to heaven. So His will would be for us to do our part that makes us qualify for heaven. It's easy - we must, by our own free will, take part in the Great Trade. Father God wants us to come to heaven, and only through participating in the Great Trade is that possible.

I found it, the Father's will, it's in John 6:40, Jesus says, "For my Father's will is that everyone who looks to the Son and believes in Him shall have eternal life, and I will raise him up on the last day."

In terms of us coming to heaven the Father's will is to look to Jesus - not to himself but to look to Jesus - and to believe in Jesus. Not just to believe that he exists, even Satan believes in God. We are to believe Jesus is who He says He is – God's son - and so God Himself - and to believe He can and will do what He says He can do. We are asked to have faith in Jesus for our salvation, and not put our faith in religion or membership or in people who believe they are the way we should follow.

We know that not everyone who believes in Jesus will go to heaven as "Not everyone who says 'Lord' will enter the kingdom of heaven."[13] We can see that this belief in Jesus is very different from just believing in God or even just believing in Jesus. This belief requires action. After all, in truth if you or I really believe that God and heaven are real and we understand and believe that Jesus is the only way to get to heaven as we must take part in the Great Trade, then certainly this belief would move us to some sort of action. This belief in Jesus that is part of the Father's will, has to be a free will belief that gets us to become actively involved in the salvation we are given when we make the Great Trade and become "in Christ and Christ in us."

I was wondering what Jesus had to say about these things, you know, the Father's will, the Great Trade, getting to have the relationship with God that we were created to have. I found His words in John 14:6 - Jesus says, "I am the way and the truth and the life. No one comes to the Father except through Me." Wow - what words of authority He speaks. Jesus says, "No one comes to the Father except through Me." The Father is in heaven, so Jesus says no one comes to heaven except through Him. You can't get to heaven through good works, and membership and sacrifice won't do. Time spent trying after death is nothing. Jesus makes it perfectly clear. He is the way, and there is no other way. He is the life - true life with God today and for eternity - and He is the truth, in a world full of lies. Jesus says that salvation and life is found only through Him, and He died on a cross and rose from the dead as proof of His words.

I'm not surprised to hear the words of Jesus, that only through participation in the Great Trade do I acquire the God righteousness that gets me right with God and into heaven as one of His very sons. Only through participation in the Great Trade are my sins given to Jesus and paid for on the cross so I don't have to pay the penalty of eternal separation from God for my sins. And only through Jesus' spirit with my spirit is this possible. Only with my spirit hooked to His spirit can I really know God's truth and God's life. Only those who are "in Christ" are not condemned.[14] Everyone else is still in their sins. Everyone else is still condemned. Everyone else has to pay their own penalty for their sins and that's eternal separation from God.

As I thought about these things I began to see why
only a few will enter into heaven. It was plain to see.
Those who decided the way to qualify to be with God
forever is to go through Jesus are successful, and
everyone else who tries to qualify to be with God in the
countless other ways will fail. I understand the trade
and so I know that this has to be. And I know God's
own perfectness and Holiness. His very love will not
take away man's free will, and it will not allow Him to
compromise on the qualifications to enter heaven in
any other way.

Then I thought, what about His chosen nation, the
Israelites, the Jews, the descendants of Abraham. This
was His nation. He must have some compromise here,
some way that these people can be saved. Saved from
their own sins and the need to pay their own penalty of
separation from God. After all these people loved
God, they worshipped at the temple and as best they
could they followed God's laws. These people wanted
God. I wondered if a chosen people who wanted God
a lot - the Bible uses the word zealous, that's very
enthusiastically wanting God - I wondered if there
might be some exception here.

I remember in my reading that the Israelite nation
mostly did not believe that Jesus was who He said He
was and in their disbelief they would not come to Jesus
for their sins forgiven and to actually have Jesus'
righteousness. They wanted to be right with God very
much. And they thought they were right with God
because of who they were as members of the chosen
nation and because they had lots of history behind

them and traditions and even the great temple of God was theirs. They had lots of things that you would expect could make them right with God, and saved from eternal destruction. Did these things save them?

The apostle Paul writes in his letter to the Romans, chapter 10 vs. 1-3, "Brothers, my heart's desire and prayer to God for the Israelites is that they may be saved. For I can testify about them that they are zealous for God, but their zeal is not based on knowledge. Since they did not know the righteousness that comes from God and sought to establish their own, they did not submit to God's righteousness." This scripture tells us that the Israelites are not saved, even though they are zealous for God they will not be with God. They don't understand that only the righteousness that comes from God, only Jesus' perfect righteousness coming to us through the Great Trade, will qualify you to go to heaven. It is the only righteousness that will save you from your own sins and the punishment that you deserve because of sin.

Lack of knowledge, lack of understanding, was not an exception in the eyes of God. With God there are no exceptions - you are righteous before Him, perfect God righteous before Him or you are not. If you are, you go to heaven - if you aren't, you don't - that's all there is. Not even being a member of a chosen nation, not even a lack of understanding, not even being zealous for God will bring an exception from God - no exceptions. No wonder Jesus said, "No one comes to the Father except through Me." A good place to start believing Jesus is to believe that He meant exactly what He said.

Alright, I've made up my mind. I believe Jesus when He says He is the only way and that no one comes to the Father except through Him. I understand the Father's will, that you turn to Jesus in trust and belief in order to receive Jesus' perfect righteousness. I have studied the scriptures and understand what they say. I also remember Jesus' word in John 5:39-40, "You diligently study the scriptures because you think that by them you possess eternal life. These are the scriptures that testify about me yet you refuse to come to Me to have life." And I remember Romans 6:23 where it says, "For the wages of sin is death, but the gift of God is eternal life in Christ Jesus our Lord."

I know that my sins have earned me eternal death yet God has a gift for me of eternal life through Jesus and the Great Trade. Jesus has life for me - life for my spirit, but in order to receive this gift of life I must come to Him. This is personal. This is very personal. Jesus and me. Its sort of funny isn't it, I wanted a personal meeting, a personal time with the president and I could never get it. But with God - to be with Him, to know Him, to spend an eternity in a relationship with Him, I need to meet with Jesus. One on one. Him and me. Jesus says I need to come to Him to have life. I believe what He says.

I'm tired of my spirit being dead. I'm tired of the heaviness of the world. I'm tired of just existing in this life. I'm tired of religion and traditions that do nothing and don't give me a relationship with God. I know that God is real. I want to know my creator. I want to know that love so great that God wants me to know

Him and sends His own Son to a cross so that the Great Trade can make things happen - so I can be one of God's sons. I want to know this God. I want to love this God. I want to serve this God. I want to be like this God.

I was created to be a spirit person, but my spirit is as dead and my flesh has taken control. My spirit needs life again. It needs to grow and produce good things for my life and for God. As my body needs food and water to grow and be healthy so also my spirit needs spiritual food, spiritual water to live and grow.

In John 6:35 Jesus declares, "I am the bread of life. He who comes to me will never go hungry and he who believes in me will never be thirsty." Jesus is speaking about life for your spirit of course - but look. Jesus says, He Himself is the very source, the very bread of life. The very source of life and nourishment for my spirit. I've noticed that my regular body gets hungry and thirsty every day and I need to take care of these basic needs every day, but Jesus is saying that He is the bread and drink of my spiritual life. Jesus is saying that I need to sort of eat and drink spiritually from him each day so my spirit lives and grows and prospers.

This personal meeting with Jesus - me and Him - this is much more than just a meeting. Much more than a one-time thing. Jesus wants me to draw life from Him. He wants to give me His perfect righteousness. He wants to put His own spirit in together with my spirit and He wants to take my spirit to be with His spirit - to the cross - to the resurrection - to heaven and to eternity with God. He wants me to

know Him - not just to know about Him, but to really
know Him. To really know the great creator Himself,
the source of all love - to know the purity and Holiness
of God. Jesus wants us to have a close, personal,
intimate relationship with Him, each and every day.

I knew religion. I knew works righteousness. I
knew traditions and doing what we do, just because we
do it. I knew fulfilling obligations. I even knew trying
to be like Jesus, and I knew being perfect was not so
easy to do. I knew that all the things I had done in my
life and all the church services I had attended had not
accomplished what had to be done to be one with God.
So far in my life I was not part of God's Great Trade. I
needed to get to Jesus.

How? How do I talk to Jesus? How do I ask Him
to trade my sins and death sentence for His
righteousness and life? How do I ask to draw strength
for my day directly from Him? How do I come to
Jesus, to God Himself in the sinful condition I'm in? I
wonder if I could sort of clean things up a bit in my life
first then go to Jesus. But I know that's hopeless. I
have no power. If I could get things cleaned up in my
life without Jesus, I wouldn't need Jesus. But I have no
power to change my life, my spirit needs to be back in
control to do that and my spirit is as dead. I need to be
born of spirit. I need to be a new creation "in Christ
and Christ in me," then I can change. I can do nothing
on my own, but that's alright, that's expected. A child
needs forgiveness, he needs help. A child needs the
strength and love of his father, and I have the right, the
very right to be God's son - Jesus did that at the cross.

I have the right to be God's son.

I know that when I talk to Jesus I'm going to start by saying "thank you," that you have made a way that me a sinner can talk to you, the Holy and pure God. How great is the honor and privilege that I can talk directly to God, to Jesus myself? In the old covenant that the people had with God, only the priest or prophets could talk to God, and only in a restricted way. But now, because Jesus is God and because of Jesus' death on the cross I am no longer an enemy of God and so I can talk to Him directly myself. In fact I must talk to Jesus myself. I can tell - my salvation is my salvation, its individual. I must go to Jesus myself. He says himself I must come - I must believe. Salvation is personal, one on one, Jesus and me.

Joseph Goldsmith

-CHAPTER 7-

It's Time to Meet Jesus

I'm back in my Bible again because I want to know more about this meeting with Jesus before I go, and I found what I was looking for, it's Romans 10:9-10. There are lots of other places in the Bible where it says just about the same thing so it's not hard to understand. It says, "That if you confess with your mouth 'Jesus is Lord' and believe in your heart that God raised Him from the dead, you will be saved. For it is with your heart that you believe and are justified, and it is with your mouth that you confess and are saved."

It says - it is with your heart that you believe and are justified. In my heart. Not in my actions or deeds, not in the things I have done or am doing. Not in the church I attend or don't attend, but it's in my heart. I know that God judges by a person's heart. I remember reading that and I know that the things in a person's heart are the things that they will live out in their lives.

I have seen people who have hatred in their hearts, it shows in their lives. And I have seen people who have love and forgiveness in their hearts and those things show in their lives as well. Sometimes a person can appear good or loving or kind, and they can be polite and respectful. But often when in a different setting things might seem a bit different and then you know what is really in that person's heart. Jesus looks at the heart.

We need to believe in our heart, not just in words or agreement, but in our heart. But believe what? I remember the Father's will - that which must be done in order to go to heaven. The Father said we must believe. We must believe that Jesus is who He says He is - that He is God - and that He can do and will do what He says He will do. That is take your sins to the cross and give you His perfect God righteousness. And Jesus says He will raise us up on the last day with Him and has prepared a spot for us to be with God in heaven. Jesus says He wants us to be one with God. To truly know God. Not just know "of" Him but to actually be one "with" Him - spirit to spirit. As we are "in Christ" and Christ is in us, we are spirit to spirit. The Father wants us to believe Jesus when He tells us these things.

Jesus says He will be our peace - our hope and strength in our day. He will love us, help us, guide us, and forgive us. He will renew us and change us to be more like He is. He will give us power over sin in our lives, and He will give us help to do these things. Help through His word, written in His Bible and help

through good Bible-based churches with church
families that will help us to have more of Him.

Jesus also says He will live in us - make us His
temple.[15] But not just that, He also says that He will live
through us - live in us and through us - for our own
lives and also to help others to see Him and know Him
and choose Him. He says He is life for us, and life for
others through us.

The Father said we must believe but remember this
is not just an "I believe in God" sort of thing. If you
really believe Jesus' words and you want forgiveness for
your sins and to be with God in heaven for your
eternity then this sort of belief would bring you to Jesus
for your salvation. This sort of trust and belief would
bring you to Jesus for a close personal relationship with
Him.

If you really believe that Jesus is God - Jesus is
creator - Jesus is king - then He will be your king. The
one you want to know, to love, to serve, to obey, the
one you worship and trust with your very life. The only
one you trust with your salvation. The one you want to
become like. The one you obey and want to learn
about and to live for. He is your strength - your peace -
your savior - your righteousness - your truth - your way
- in fact He is your very life. Not just a source of life.
Not just a part of your life. Jesus wants to become your
life. To live in you and through you as a father lives in
his son and through his son so does Jesus want to live
in you and through you. He wants to give you the
greatest life that is possible for you to live - a life with
Jesus. And through you He wants to help others to

choose life for themselves - to choose Jesus.

This is the hope of Jesus. This is the will of the Father. To believe in your heart that Jesus is God and creator and savior. A belief that demands change and action. A belief that brings you to Jesus. A new beginning. A new life. A new creation - in Christ - Christ in you.

And you need to believe, to believe in your heart that God raised Jesus from the dead. Jesus is alive. He lives to intercede for us[16] - to love us and to help us to bring others willing to be with Him into heaven. Jesus lives so that He can live in us and live through us. After all, a dead God is no God at all. A dead God can't love you, hear your prayers or care about your life.

Jesus paid my penalty. He went to the cross for me. He suffered on that cross and He had separation from the Father and He died. The things needed for God to make the trade were accomplished - all put into place. The full price had been paid. Jesus had done His part. He had given up His perfectness and innocence to take for himself the pain and punishment that our sin demands. Father God had made the trade. Now Jesus needs to live again - to be our God. Jesus needs to be raised from the dead. He needs to be perfect again, Holy and righteous again, our hope and source of life.[17] Jesus needs to be returned to His perfect relationship with the Father and so He is raised from the dead in Glory and power and righteousness and Holiness.

Jesus lives to bring those who are children of God - those who qualify for the inheritance of heaven - He lives to raise them from the dead and to bring them to heaven to be forever with himself. Yes, Jesus is alive that we may be alive in Christ. I absolutely believe it in my heart - Jesus rose from the dead.

It was time - it was past time. I wanted to know this God of love. This God that I had such great value to that He would die on a cross for me. I wanted to know Him personally. I wanted to call His name. I wanted to talk to Him and have Him listen and then talk to me. I wanted to experience His perfect love and His grace and favor on my life. And I wanted to love Him. This God who loves me so much - I wanted to love Him.

I admit that I hadn't said a prayer to God for so long that I wasn't even sure that He really existed. But my spirit was sure - or my heart. Something inside of me seemed so empty and it was as if it cried out for life itself. My mind seemed hooked to the world, to no God and evolution instead. But inside, inside there was a growing feeling, a desperation - a great need to talk to God. A great need to get to Jesus.

Each day my young friend would ask me if I had talked with God the night before - did I say a prayer? The answer was, "no." I had been away from God for a very long time and to even say one word to God, my Creator, seemed very hard to do. I admit that it seems a bit strange but all during these days I could feel His love for me. It was strong and felt very nice and it gave me a sort of peace inside of me. Yet I had not spoken to Him.

My mind kept questioning - who is this God that I have such value to that He loves me even when I don't speak to Him, and don't love Him back?

I've noticed that my mind and my heart don't often seem to think in the same way - I expect that's why Jesus looks at the heart. I decided to let my heart be in control.

I took a couple of deep breaths and tears began to fill my eyes and drop to the floor. I knelt down at the foot of my bed because I really didn't know what to do or what to say. I could feel His love so strong, so powerful. His presence seemed to fill the room. Mostly I just knelt there with my head down and cried, and I said thank you - thank you for your love. Thank you for your cross. Thank you for coming for me in the fields. As I felt a peace come over me and became a little more bold in my talk with Jesus - this God who creates trillions of stars - I couldn't help but ask Him, why? Why do you love me? Why do I have value to you? This world doesn't love me and I have no real value to any part of the world. Why?

My mind was full of thoughts and confusion as I sort of tried to answer my own question. There was a mix of several things going on in my mind when suddenly one thought seemed so strong, so clear, so bold. The thought was, "I am your Father" - this was not my thought. This was not even my consideration. I was trying to think on things a bit and admitted to myself that that was a nice thought wherever it came from. Suddenly a new thought seemed to push its way to the front. Bold and clear, I almost seem to hear the words as if spoken out loud, "You are my son." As I'm still trying to understand things a third time in my mind I hear the words of God - "You belong to me."

I didn't understand the fullness of what God meant by these words but I knew that things were different in my life now. My bedroom still looked the same. I still had the same job and so many other things were still the same. But I just didn't feel empty inside anymore. I didn't feel worthless and I didn't feel unloved. I had value, real value, to the almighty God. I was loved by Jesus. I had gone to Jesus and I had made the trade. I was born again - a son of God.

My life belonged to Jesus now. In truth I was a bit surprised he wanted my life as it seemed pretty much worthless to me. I was happy that my life no longer belonged to the world, to other people, or even to me. I expected it was going to need a lot of repair work - healing, unlearning things and learning new things, forgiveness as I grow in Christ and change. And I was right, the first year that I belonged to Jesus was a hard year. I did a lot of crying that year but Jesus taught me how to draw strength from Him each day, and He taught me how to live out that these painful things of the world - these things are not my life - Jesus is my life.

I wish I could tell you how great it is to be alive "in Christ." For so many years of my life I simply existed, I lived but I was not really alive. I existed in the world with no spirit to spirit connection to God. I lived by the world and by my flesh and not by God and my spirit. To live with Jesus is a change that is so great - so wonderful - but I can't really explain it to you. You must experience it yourself, personally - one on one - you and Jesus.

Feeling a bit empty in your life today? I know why,

it's because you are empty in your life. Do you have days that it seems you are just existing and not really alive - you need to be born again. For those of you who attend a church and really do want to know God, are you tired of religion with no real relationship with Jesus? Are you sick of trying to perform obligations and works in order to make it into heaven? Are you discouraged with leaders who say they can get you to heaven if you follow their ways yet talk of things that must be done even after you are dead? Are you dissatisfied with not knowing for sure, in your own heart and in your own spirit, that you will be forever with God? Are you sick of the emptiness that is in your heart and spirit and sick of trying to fill that hole with things of the world?

Well then it's time - it's past time. Make the trade - become one with Jesus. From your heart, talk to Jesus. Ask Him to be your savior. To be your source of life and strength. Ask Him to forgive your sins and help you to live for righteousness. Thank Him for His sacrifice on the cross for you. Tell Him that you make Him your Lord and King. Tell Him that you love Him and thank Him for His great love for you. And give Him your life. Yes, give Him your life - to live in and live through. To change and heal and correct. Your life for Him to use to bring others to himself, your life to bring glory to God.

As you say these things to Jesus with your lips, out loud, as you would talk to a person and from your heart, I am sure that there will be other things that you wish to say as well. And don't forget to listen. God speaks into your mind and into your heart and He will answer your words to Him.

It says in 2 Corinthians 5:5   that God actually created us for the very purpose of being with Him forever and that He has given us the spirit - that's Jesus' spirit - the Holy Spirit - as a deposit guaranteeing what is to come. I had said that I wanted a guarantee about going to heaven, well, what can be better than the very spirit of God Himself joined as one to your spirit so at the time of death you can go instantly to be with Jesus.

As for me - I made the Great Trade 15 years ago and another guarantee of my eternity is the continual presence of God in my life. His love, His grace, His hope and peace. His comfort and strength in trials and painful times as well as in wonderful days. He is with me now and I feel it, and know it, and so I will be with Him forever.

I urge you to make the trade - make Jesus your Lord and Savior. Then get into a good Bible based church. The people and leaders can help you to renew your mind to the thoughts of God. They can help in your transition to a new life and help you to have more of Jesus in your life. Be sure that the church you choose is helping you to have more of Jesus - a stronger relationship with God - not religion and works and a relationship with them.

Be Blessed - I will greet you in heaven. - Joe

-FOOTNOTES-

1 – 1 Corinthians 15:33

2 – Genesis 1:1

3 – Genesis 2:17, Genesis 3:6

4 – Numbers 14, Deuteronomy 1-2, Joshua 1

5 – Romans 3:20

6 – Isaiah 64:6

7 – 1 John 4:8

8 – Romans 3:23

9 – Matthew 27:46

10 – Ephesians 1:4, 1 Peter 1:18-20

11 – Ephesians 1:13-14, Hebrews 9:15, Romans 8:14-16

12 – Romans 8:13

13 – Matthew 7:21

14 – Romans 8:1

15 – 1 Corinthians 3:16

16 – 1 Timothy 2:5

17 – Hebrews 2:10

All scripture references refer to the New International Version Study Bible, 10th Anniversary Edition. Copyright 1995, The Zondervan Corporation.

-ABOUT THE AUTHOR-

Joseph Goldsmith is a member of the New Life Community Church in Amery, Wisconsin. He teaches Bible Studies and is active in prayer, missions and evangelism.

A Veterinarian by trade, Doc Joe always enjoys time spent in occupational evangelism and individual discipleship. He is an ordained minister of Impact Ministries International and has been working and ministering for many years with families and orphans in Comayagua, Honduras.

Doc Joe can be reached by e-mail at drjoe@amerytel.net